CLASSICAL COMPOSERS

Franz Joseph HAYDN

by Joanne Mattern
with Consultation by John Viscardi,
Executive Director of Classic Lyric Arts
illustrated by Marilena Perilli

Egremont, Massachusetts

Classical Composers has been produced and published by Red Chair Press Books for Young Readers:
Red Chair Press LLC PO Box 333 South Egremont, MA 01258
www.redchairpress.com

 Download a Free Activity Guide on our website.

For more information about Classic Lyric Arts, visit www.classiclyricarts.org.

Names: Mattern, Joanne, 1963- author. | Viscardi, John, consultant. | Perilli, Marilena, illustrator.

Title: Franz Joseph Haydn / by Joanne Mattern, with consultation by John Viscardi, executive director of Classic Lyric Arts ; illustrated by Marilena Perilli.

Description: Egremont, Massachusetts : Red Chair Press, [2026] | Series: Mattern, Joanne, 1963- Classical composers. | Interest age level: 008-012. | Includes bibliographical references and index. | Summary: Franz Joseph Haydn (1732–1809) was an influential Austrian composer of the Classical era. Known as the "Father of the Symphony" and "Father of the String Quartet," he helped shape classical music's structure and style still used today.--Publisher.

Identifiers: LCCN: 2025939514 | ISBN: 9781967893065 (library hardcover) | 9781967893072 (paperback) | 9781967893096 (S&L ePub 3) | 9781967893089 (S&L ebook PDF) | 9781967893119 (audiobook)

Subjects: LCSH: Haydn, Joseph, 1732-1809--Juvenile literature. | Composers--Austria--Biography--Juvenile literature. | CYAC: Haydn, Joseph, 1732-1809. | Composers--Austria--Biography. | LCGFT: Biographies. | BISAC: JUVENILE NONFICTION / Music / Classical. | JUVENILE NONFICTION / Biography & Autobiography / Music. | JUVENILE NONFICTION / Biography & Autobiography / Performing Arts.

Classification: LCC: ML410.H4 M38 2026 | DDC: 780.92--dc23

Image credits: 4 Bridgeman Images; 6 Ernst Hader/Courtesy of the Wien Museum; 12 Rudolf Hoffman/Courtesy of the Wien Museum; 16 © NPL - DeA Picture Library/Bridgeman Images; 18 Bridgeman Images; 24 Chronicle/Alamy; 25 MP_Foto/Shutterstock; 30 Gacro74/Alamy

Illustrations: Marilena Perilli, except p. 7 by Joe LeMonnier

Printed in the United States of America

0426 1P F26CG

Table of Contents

A New Kind of Music

Franz Joseph Haydn was a famous **composer**. He created a new kind of music. Haydn's work **influenced** composers who came after him. He changed classical music in a big way!

Talented Boy

Franz Joseph Haydn was born on March 31, 1732. He was born in a small town called Rohrau in Austria. His father made wheels for carriages. His mother was a cook for the lord of Rohrau.

The little boy was called by his middle name. Joseph was the second of twelve children. But only five of his siblings lived to adulthood. That was not uncommon in those days.

North Sea
DENMARK
SWEDEN
Copenhagen
Baltic Sea
HANOVER
PRUSSIA
Berlin
POLISH-
LITHUANIAN
COMMONWEALTH
U.P.
SAXONY
SMALL
GERMAN
STATES
Prague
BOHEMIA
Hainburg
Rohrau
BAVARIA
AUSTRIA
HUNGARY
FRANCE
SWITZERLAND
SARDINIA
VENICE
OTTOMAN
EMPIRE
PAPAL STATES

As a little boy, Joseph loved music. He had a beautiful singing voice. When Joseph was six years old, his uncle, Johann Matthias, visited the Haydns. Johann Matthias was a choirmaster in a town called Hainburg.

When he heard Joseph sing, Johann Matthias offered to train the boy as a musician. Joseph's parents agreed. When he was just six years old, Joseph moved to Hainburg to live with his uncle.

B# **B SHARP:** Joseph's brother Michael Haydn is known as one of the best composers of church music.

When Joseph was eight years old, he joined the **choir** at St. Stephen's Cathedral in Vienna, Austria. Vienna was the capital of Austria, and St. Stephen's was its most important church.

Joseph lived at St. Stephen's for eight years. He went to the choir school. Joseph learned a lot about music. He studied other subjects too. Life at St. Stephen's was a lot of work. But Joseph enjoyed the music!

A New Beginning

By the time Haydn was sixteen, his voice had changed. He could no longer sing high notes. He also got in trouble for cutting off another boy's hair as a prank. Haydn was asked to leave the choir. He had to leave the school as well.

Haydn did not know what to do. He had no money and no job. Fortunately, a friend took him in. He lived in the friend's attic and worked odd jobs.

Haydn was determined to be a musician. He listened to every kind of music he could. He taught himself about famous composers and their works. Haydn also taught music to children. He did not have a lot of money, but he was happy.

One day, Haydn met a man named Nicola Porpora. Porpora was a composer and singing teacher. He hired Haydn to be his accompanist. Haydn played music while Porpora's students sang.

B#

B SHARP: One of Porpora's students was a young woman named Marianna Martines. She would go on to become a well-known composer herself.

Music Director

In 1759, Haydn's luck got even better. He was hired as the Kapellmeister, or music director, for the Count of Bohemia. One of Haydn's jobs was to lead the **orchestra**. Haydn wrote his first **symphony** for the orchestra to play.

The count and his court liked Haydn's music. It sounded fresh and lively. Haydn's music was simpler than the complex music of the time. But it also had emotions that made people feel happy or sad.

B# **B SHARP:** At this time, most **noble** families had their own orchestras and singers to entertain the family and their guests.

A Dream Job

Unfortunately, the Count did not have enough money to pay his orchestra. All the musicians lost their jobs. So did Haydn. Along with his salary, Haydn lost his home. But he stayed cheerful. He believed something good would happen. And it did!

Haydn was soon hired by a family called the Esterházys. The Esterházys were rich and powerful. And they loved music! Prince Anton, the head of the Esterházys, asked Haydn to be his assistant **conductor**. Haydn said yes!

Haydn had a lot to do. He helped conduct Prince Anton's orchestra. He led rehearsals and gave lessons to the singers. Haydn also composed lots of music for the orchestra to play.

The Esterházys loved Haydn. So did the musicians. Haydn was always cheerful and polite. He got along with people. Haydn loved his job. He would work for the Esterházy family for the next 30 years.

B#

B SHARP: Haydn got married in 1760. But the marriage was not a happy one. His wife hated music. She even used some of Haydn's music to line her baking sheets!

B♯ **B SHARP:** Haydn became good friends with another composer. His name was Wolfgang Amadeus Mozart. Mozart even called his friend "Papa Haydn."

Prince Anton died in 1762. His brother, Prince Nikolaus, became the new family leader. Nikolaus loved music even more than Anton did. He encouraged Haydn to write all kinds of music. Haydn composed **operas** and symphonies. He wrote **string quartets** too.

Haydn Becomes Famous

Haydn produced a lot of music for the Esterházys. Soon, people in other countries heard Haydn's music as well. He sold copies of his music to **monasteries**. He sold them to other noble families too. Haydn's music became popular all over Europe.

The Esterházy family were at one time the largest landowners in present day Austria, Slovakia, and Hungary. Esterházy Palace (shown) in Eisenstadt, Austria was the family home for more than 300 years.

In 1790, Prince Nikolaus died. His son did not like music very much. He fired all of his musicians except Haydn. He told Haydn he could stay or go.

Haydn was soon lonely at the Esterházy estate. He missed Vienna and his friends there. So Haydn moved to Vienna. But before he could get settled, he got an offer to go to London. Haydn accepted. In London, he wrote and conducted six symphonies, an opera, and many other works. Even the royal family came to see his performances.

In 1795, Haydn returned to Vienna. He went back to work for the Esterházys. During that time, he wrote six Masses. These are among his most famous works.

In 1798, Haydn wrote a famous **oratorio**. It was called *The Creation*. The oratorio was written in both German and English.

Haydn's last years were quiet ones. He died in his sleep on May 31, 1809. He was 77 years old. But the music composed by the man people fondly called "Papa Haydn" would live on for hundreds of years after his death.

B#

B SHARP: Haydn invited Ludwig van Beethoven to come to Vienna to study with him. But the two did not get along.

A strange thing happened after Haydn died. Thieves stole his head after Haydn was buried. Haydn's skull was not recovered for another 75 years. It was reburied with his body. Haydn loved practical jokes. Many people think he would have found the story of his missing head quite funny.

Haydn's tomb in Eisenstadt, Austria.

Important Dates in Franz Joseph Haydn's Life

1732 Franz Joseph Haydn is born in Rohrau, Austria, on March 31.

1738 Haydn moves to Hainburg to live with his uncle.

1740 Haydn joins the choir at St. Stephen's Cathedral in Vienna.

1748 Haydn is forced to leave St. Stephen's.

1766 Haydn becomes the music director for the Esterházy family.

1791 Haydn visits London for the first time.

1795 Haydn comes home to Vienna to work again for the Esterházy family.

1798 Haydn composes his famous oratorio, *The Creation.*

1809 Haydn dies on May 31.

Glossary

choir a group of people who sing together, often in a church or school

composer a person who writes music

conductor a person who leads an orchestra

influenced had an effect on someone

monasteries buildings where men called monks live under religious vows

noble belonging to a high social class

Opera An art form where stories are told by singers performing on a stage accompanied by instrumentalists

oratorio a work for singers and instruments, usually with a theme from the Bible

orchestra a group of instruments playing together

string quartets a musical group made up of a cello, viola, and two violins

symphony long pieces of music for an orchestra

Read More About Haydn

Summerer, Eric Michael. *Franz Joseph Haydn.* PowerKids Press, 2006.

Zannos, Susan. *The Life and Times of Franz Joseph Haydn.* Mitchell Lane Publishers, 2004.

Index